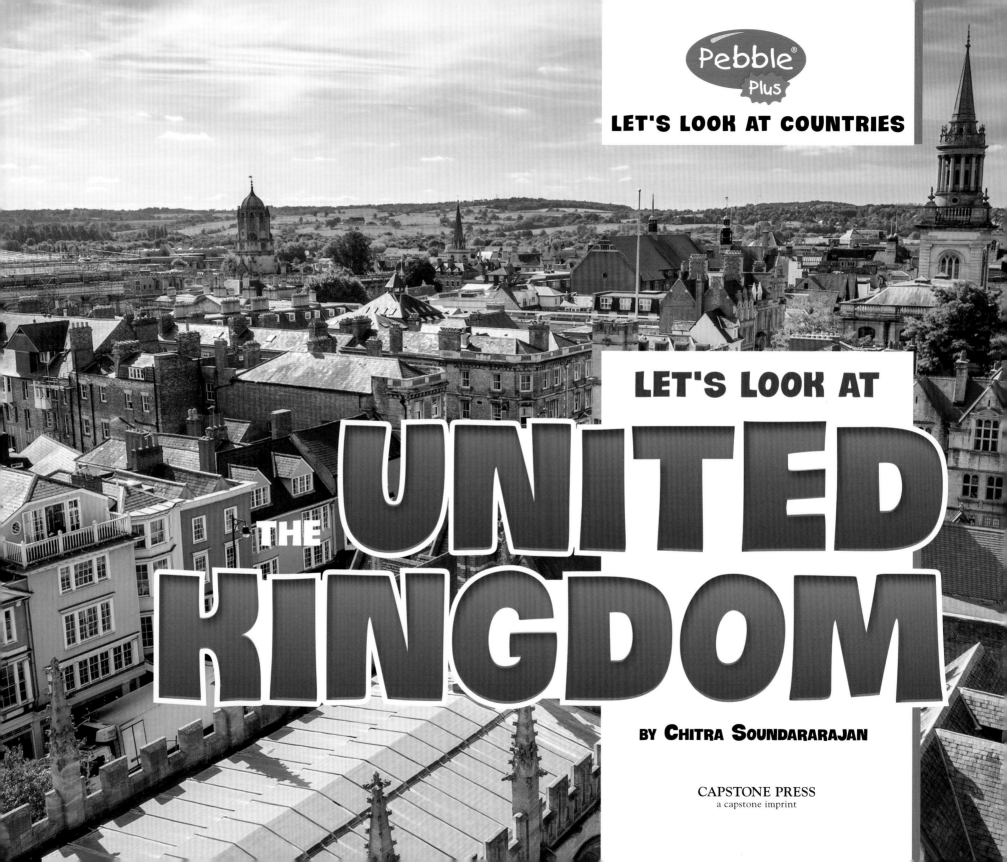

Pebble® Plus

LET'S LOOK AT COUNTRIES

LET'S LOOK AT

THE UNITED KINGDOM

BY CHITRA SOUNDARARAJAN

CAPSTONE PRESS
a capstone imprint

Pebble Plus is published by Capstone Press,
1710 Roe Crest Drive, North Mankato, Minnesota 56003
www.mycapstone.com

Library of Congress Cataloging-in-Publication Data
Names: Soundararajan, Chitra, author.
Title: Let's look at the United Kingdom / by Chitra Soundararajan.
Description: Pebble : North Mankato, Minnesota, 2020. | Series: Pebble plus.
Let's look at countries | Audience: Grades K-3. | Audience: Ages 4-8.
Identifiers: LCCN 2019001960| ISBN 9781543572148 (hardcover) |
ISBN 9781543574760 (pbk.) | ISBN 9781543572285 (ebook pdf)
Subjects: LCSH: Great Britain—Juvenile literature.
Classification: LCC DA27.5 .S64 2020 | DDC 941—dc23
LC record available at https://lccn.loc.gov/2019001960

Editorial Credits
Jessica Server, editor; Juliette Peters, designer; Jo Miller, media researcher;
Laura Manthe, production specialist

Photo Credits
Alamy: South West Images Scotland, 14-15; Newscom: Blend Images/ERproductions Ltd, 17;
Shutterstock: Andrei Nekrassov, 1, AR Pictures, Cover Top, Bartosz Luczak, 12, Bildagentur Zoonat
GmbH, 2-3, Chris Allen, 20-21, Chris Harvey, 11, Globe Turner, 22 (Inset), Kasefoto, 6-7, Mark Caunt,
8, Milosz Maslanka, 22-23, 24, Mistervlad, 4-5, Monkey Business Images, 16, nale, 4 (map), neil
langan, 13, Nicola Pulham, 9, Peter Titmuss, 18-19, Sara Winter, Cover Middle, Simon Baylis, Cover
Bottom, Cover Back

All internet sites appearing in back matter were available and accurate when this book
was sent to press.

Note to Parents and Teachers

The Let's Look at Countries set supports national curriculum standards for social studies related
to people, places, and culture. This book describes and illustrates the United Kingdom. The images
support early readers in understanding the text. The repetition of words and phrases helps early
readers learn new words. This book also introduces early readers to subject-specific vocabulary
words, which are defined in the Glossary section. Early readers may need assistance to read some
words and to use the Table of Contents, Glossary, Read More, Internet Sites, Critical Thinking
Questions, and Index sections of the book.

Printed and bound in China.
1654

TABLE OF CONTENTS

Where Is the United Kingdom?

The United Kingdom is in Europe. It includes England, Scotland, Wales, Northern Ireland, and many smaller islands. Its capital is London.

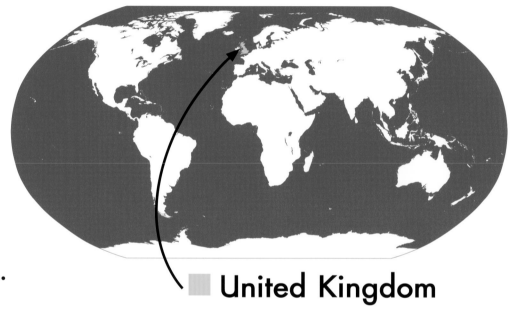

United Kingdom

London

From Coasts to Mountains

Coasts surround the United Kingdom. Mountains stand in the north and the west. Ben Nevis is the tallest mountain in Scotland. Snowdon is the tallest mountain in Wales.

Ben Nevis

In the Wild

The United Kingdom has many animals. Fox and deer run in the woods. Atlantic puffins catch fish in the ocean. Seals rest on beaches.

fox

seals

People

Many British people have ancestors from Europe. Others traveled from Asia, Africa, and the Caribbean. Most British people speak English. People in Wales speak Welsh.

At the Table

People in the United Kingdom enjoy fish and chips. Welsh cakes are a treat in Wales. Many people like to drink black tea with milk, sugar, or lemon.

Welsh cakes

fish and chips

Festivals

Scottish people celebrate Burns Night in January. This festival honors the poet Robert Burns. In fall, people around the United Kingdom celebrate Diwali, the festival of lights.

Burns Night carnival

On the Job

Many British people used to work in manufacturing. Today most British people work in service jobs. This includes plumbers, bankers, teachers, and many other jobs.

Transportation

People travel by cars, trains, and ferries. Ferries are boats that carry people and cars short distances. Trains run under the sea to other places in Europe.

Famous Site

Stonehenge is an ancient monument.

It is a circle of large stones.

Stonehenge is around 5,000 years

old. Around 1 million people visit it

each year.

QUICK UK FACTS

United Kingdom's flag

Name: United Kingdom of Great Britain and Northern Ireland

Capital: London

Other major cities: Edinburgh, Cardiff, Belfast

Population: 65,105,246 (July 2018 estimate)

Size: 94,058 square miles (243,610 sq km)

Language: English

Money: Great British pound

GLOSSARY

ancestor—a family member who lived a long time ago

capital—the city in a country where the government is based

chips—thickly cut potato strips, fried in hot oil

honor—to give praise or show respect

manufacturing—process of making products

monument—a statue or building that is meant to remind people of an event or a person

poet—a person who writes poems